Awakening

Divine Love

JOURNAL

Jewels of Light Publishing
14300 NE 20th St
Ste D 102-383
Vancouver, WA 98686
1.855.50 JEWEL (505.3935)
JewelsofLight.com

Cover Design and Interior Design
by Deborah Perdue, Illumination Graphics

ISBN: 978-1893037-10-6

Jewels of Light Publishing©
Copyright 2013

Awakening Dvine Love Journal

 *Jewels* is the founder of the Jewels of Light Experience, and she is a seasoned energy medicine practitioner who has been working in energy healing for the past 20 years.

She offers transformational energy healing sessions through guidance and counseling. Her sessions offer an invitation to transcend personal limitations so we may increase our capacity of compassion, understanding, love and grace.

Her dynamic educational energy medicine course, The Life Essence Awakening Process is used worldwide by energy medicine practitioners. Jewels is the author of six books which educate on healing, spiritual practice and energy medicine. The Jewels of Light Experience offers inspirational books, artwork, gifts, sacred body care, ascension yoga apparel and uplifting workshops and events.

The company is founded in love and our connection to our sacred source. She is delighted to share her essential wisdom at this paramount time in our existence. For more information about Jewels work and the Jewels of Light Experience, please visit JewelsofLight. com or email Jewels@jewelsoflight.com . NAMASTE

In the beginning,
In the time before time begins,
In the rest before movement begins,
In the peace where nothing but
Elobim is, was and will be.
It all unfolds and moves like the wings
of a bird taking flight,
like a spark turning to flame,
spreading the fire in all directions.
From this center, everything travels toward
its purpose, somehow moving together and yet,
each with its own kernel
of destiny known only to the Holy one.

Gen, 1:1a B'reshrath
From Genesis Meditations
Neal Douglas Klotz

Wisdom

Within you there is an innate, divine intelligence that is rarely touched. This divine intelligence is the supreme intelligence, untainted by thought, memory, and time, stemming from the universal source of the infinite.

By letting go of what is untrue, can I learn to truly live?

Are you ready to accept your Soul's calling?
Begin by listening to the voice of the silence
within, surrendering to the divine guidance of truth
and wisdom.

Turning within, will you meet your true nature?

Unconditional Acceptance

The invitation is to embrace all of life with calm
equanimity, knowing from the wisdom of your heart
that all is subject to change; it is here you refer back to
the unchanging nature of stillness.

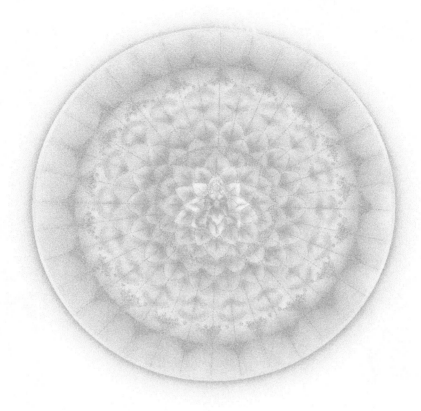

Living in Surrender

Recognizing that there is only pure consciousness is to surrender to the peace, light and silence of your awareness.

Awakening

*The awakened being quietly listens,
trusting in the source of
its being and the sacred movement of life.*

Can grace guide you to understand and heal the cause of sorrow?

Where can I find the miracle of truth?

Awakening

*The awakened being is guided to the sacred and clears
all illusions, conditions and patterns that have
obscured right viewing.*

Awareness

The root cause of the loss of self can always be traced back to the belief in separation. Integrated awareness is seeing that your happiness is found by bringing the attention back to silence—the nature of the true self.

What is suffering other than a state of separation and misidentification?

Beyond Conditioning

The nature of consciousness is observation. All is seen as passing clouds in the sky. Knowing that you are an eternal being, free from identification, will allow all to pass freely through your consciousness.

Living in Balance

Your true nature is not subject to duality, the process of birth and death, or time. It is always present in silence and is infused by the sacred energy of life.

Beauty

*Beauty is living in grace, fully appreciating
and seeing goodness
in this manifested world.*

What will you find when you turn to the light of your true nature?

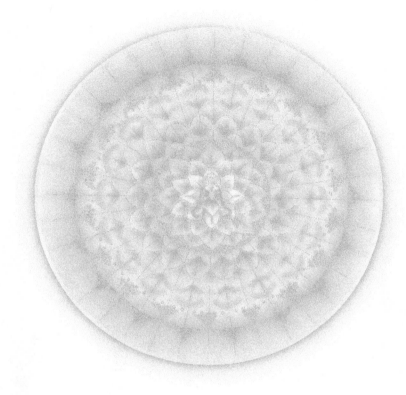

Service

*Being in the moment, free from entanglements
of the past, is holding the intention for service.
Awareness is born from the love of your true
nature; service is applying this love to whatever
life presents. Service is simply living in your truth,
and shining the light of your true nature.*

Beauty

*All of the beauty of life is found within. As
you live from your wholeness, you are one
with the magnificent oceans, the splendid
array of nature, the grandness of this
earth's unfathomable beauty.*

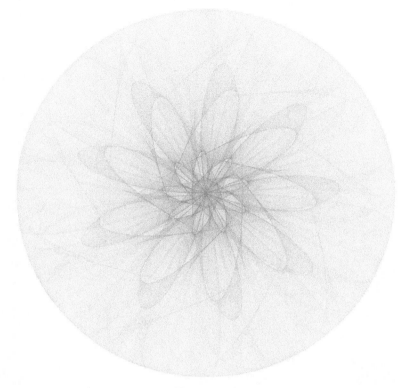

Beauty

*You are the beauty of the sea, where the wave
knows its source is the ocean itself. You are the grandeur
of the mountain, knowing that the first step up the
mountain is the same as the arrival. You are the love in
a child's heart, knowing that wonder and innocence is
your true nature. You are the beauty of your daily life,
where each moment is precious when lived to the tune
of your celestial song.*

What does it mean to truly and unconditionally love yourself?

Compassion

Compassionate seeing is viewing all that appears with an unconditional heart and open mind, accepting all in the flow of consciousness. In this way of seeing, there is total honesty, total acceptance of "what is," and a possibility of transformation.

Courage

Living with courage is holding the intention to be free from needless personal sorrow and to no longer contribute to the sorrow of humanity.

What does a courageous soul see?

Devotion

Love is the essence of pure consciousness, deepening as you unfold into the light of your true self. To love yourself is to love the eternal sacred force that is your true self; from this love comes the love of the divine. To love yourself is to recognize the living divinity within, seeing that there is only oneness in truth.

What is beauty to you?

Discernment

Living in discernment is to be firmly planted in witness consciousness, seeing and observing the nature of your temporary thoughts and emotions. Discernment comes from your inner wisdom, with the strong intention to live according to the voice of your true nature.

Forgiveness

Forgiveness of yourself and others is having the compassion to understand that mistakes are made from the illusory self, and there is never any harm meant. All comes from ignorance when you walk in the mistaken identity of the self. All is forgiven when you turn to the light of your true nature.

What is your true reality?

The Sacred River of Grace

Grace is the sacred river behind all of life. It flows in its mysterious way through your lifetime, guiding you, assisting you in the revelation of true reality. All of life's difficulties are disguised in grace. Each painful experience leads you closer to your eternal stillness of truth and wisdom, healing the cause of sorrow.

Can the mind be silent?

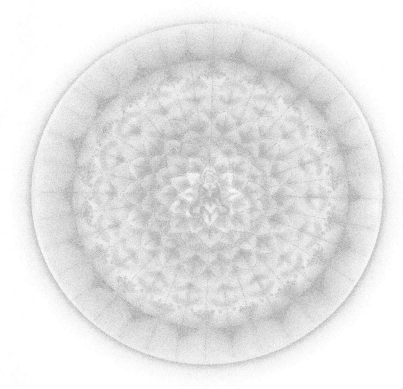

Gratitude

Gratitude is a natural blossoming and understanding of your true nature. Life becomes a daily blessing, pointing to the true source of your being.

Happiness and Joy

Happiness is a simple state of pure being, the state before Thought and before waking, a place where there is no effort. You are the very essence of happiness and joy, for what is behind all of your thoughts, emotions and physical sensations is the flow of life itself, which is pure happiness. In your truest being, you are a song of joy to the divine, rejoicing in the simplest display of life, the beauty that is before you.

Will I be free from my sense of separation?

Silence of Being

Listen quietly within, where it is possible to perceive the emptiness of this vast universe, knowing that all of creation appears from immaculate stillness.

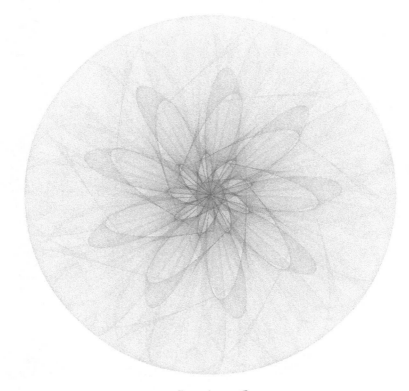

Letting Go

The art of letting go is seeing clearly that your true nature is revealed only in freedom, where you no longer hold on to the past. In letting go and releasing the past, you learn to truly live in the moment, giving yourself to life and being fully present.

What do you want from life?

The Light of the Soul

When we cease to identify with the ego-self, which is the source of separation, we open the channel for the light of the soul and return to our natural state of unity.

What comes from sacred silence?

The Timeless Flow of Life

All human beings are graced with wisdom and
the ability to contemplate the real meaning of life,
seeing that in truth you are a free being, flowing
down life's timeless river.

In the centre of the castle of Brahman,
our own body, there is a small shrine in the form of
a lotus~flower, and within can be found a small
space. We should find who dwells there,
and we should want to know him.

And if anyone asks,
"Who is he who dwells in a small shrine
in the form of a lotus~flower
in the centre of the castle of Brahman?
Whom should we want to find and to know?"

We can answer~ "The little space within
the heart is as great as this vast universe.
The heavens and the earth are there,
and the sun, and the moon, and the stars, fire and
lightning and winds are there, and all that is and
all that is not…for the whole universe is in Him
and He dwells within our heart."

Chandogya Upanishad

Is the gateway always open?

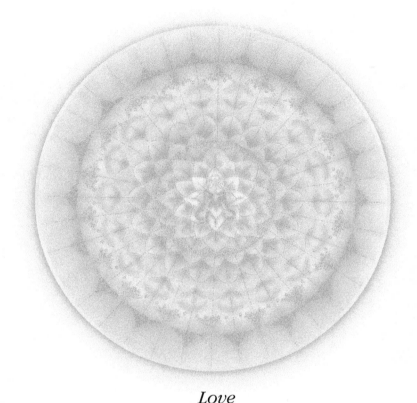

Love

*Love is seeing the truth in yourself and in others,
understanding all is one. Love is inclusive without
judgment, accepting and embracing all. For in loving
"what is," there is an immense freedom to be of service.*

What is the foundation of truth?

Peace

*Knowing your true nature, you can return to your
source at any time and experience a nurturing
of the peace and quiet within you. The beauty of life
is that, in each moment, there is a new opportunity for
this return.*

Am I conditioned by who I think I am?

The Essential Question~ Who Am I?

Look into the nature of your true self and all that you are not will fall away, revealing the immense light of your true Being.

Mistaken Identity

*The moment there is a meeting with your
eternal true nature, the end of worldly
identification occurs, and the realization
happens that you are one with all of life. All
sense of separation dissolves in this oneness; the
spark of your divinity now shines.*

Attention to Silence

Silence is the foundation for truth, and the temporary nature of life is displayed. Turning within, to the silence of your true nature, you will have access to unlimited love, wisdom and joy.

Can I find my true nature within my heart?

Jewels

offers guidance on how to tap into the magnificent being that you are. During this time of evolutionary awakening, we are guided to take a step into our divine potential. Jewels invites you to take this step and enter the temple of your inner light, where you are simply asked to let go of all that is prohibiting you from experiencing your radiant being.

OWN THE JEWELS OF LIGHT SERIES & PRODUCTS

Book 1: Well Being - Body, Mind & Spirit
Book 2: The Path of Return
Book 3: Trust In Yourself
Book 4: Living Meditations
Awakening Your Chakras
(Hard & Soft cover - with full color illustrations)

ADDITIONAL BOOKS:
Life Essence Awakening Energy Medicine Manual

PRODUCTS:
Individual Chakra Posters • Kundalini Chakra Poster
Reference Charts • Jewels Happiness Poster
Chakra Blessing Oracle Deck • Chakra Jeweled Greeting Cards
Coordinated Bookmarks • Chakra Note Cards • Gemstones
Essential Oils • Chakra Pendulums & Jewelry • Chakra Spa Line

PLUS...
Books • Seminar Information
Videos • Audio Books
eBooks • Calendar of Events
Charts & Posters • Free Downloads
Training & Education • And More!

www.JewelsofLight.com • or www.jayasarada.com
Or call toll free: 1.855.50 JEWEL (505.3935)

CPSIA information can be obtained
at www.ICGtesting.com
Printed in the USA
FFHW022341261018
48926307-53171FF

9 781893 037106